Tim Price

For Once

Methuen Drama

Published by Methuen Drama 2011

Methuen Drama, an imprint of Bloomsbury Publishing Plc

1 3 5 7 9 10 8 6 4 2

Methuen Drama
Bloomsbury Publishing Plc
36 Soho Square
London W1D 3QY
www.methuendrama.com

First published by Methuen Drama in 2011

Commissioned and first performed by Pentabus Theatre

The author has asserted his rights under the Copyright, Designs
and Patents Act 1988 to be identified as the author of this work.

ISBN: 978 1 408 15872 2

A CIP catalogue record for this book is available from the British Library

Available in the USA from Bloomsbury Academic & Professional, 175 Fifth
Avenue/3rd Floor, New York, NY 10010. www.BloomsburyAcademicUSA.com

Typeset by Mark Heslington Ltd, Scarborough, North Yorkshire

PENTABUS THEATRE

presents the world premiere

of

FOR ONCE

BY

TIM PRICE

Originally commissioned by Pentabus Theatre

First performed at Hampstead Theatre,

Michael Frayn Space 8th July 2011

FOR ONCE
by Tim Price

The Company

April	**Geraldine Alexander**
Gordon	**Patrick Driver**
Sid	**Jonathan Smith**
Director	**Orla O'Loughlin**
Designer	**Anthony Lamble**
Lighting Designer	**Philip Gladwell**
Sound Designer	**Christopher Shutt**
Assistant Director	**Ben Webb**
Production Manager	**Chris Bagust**
Technical Stage Manager	**Lorna Adamson**
Set Builder	**Rob Hill**
Assistant Stage Manager	**Jess Jackson**
Assistant Stage Manager	**Hannah Turner**

Special thanks to:
Paul S. Cannon (Consultant Ophthalmic Surgeon), Frances Kraus at the Candle Project, Emporos of Ludlow, Paws and Claws of Ludlow, Homecare of Ludlow, Ludlow Food Centre, Tesco and The Co-operative, Duncan Trew, Phil Sams, Neil Church, Malcolm Farrar, Paul Curran.

GERALDINE ALEXANDER: April

Recent theatre includes: *In Praise of Love* **(Royal and Derngate)**; *Fabrication* **(The Print Room)**; *State of Emergency* **(Gate Theatre)**; *Fall* **(Traverse Theatre,** Edinburgh); *Holy Terror* **(Tour & West End)**; *Titus Andronicus, A Midsummer Night's Dream, The Tempest* and *The Two Noble Kinsmen* **(Globe Theatre)**; *Pillars of the Community* **(National Theatre)** *Inconceivable* **(West Yorkshire Playhouse)**;*The Seagull, A Woman of No Importance* and *Present Laughter* **(Royal Exchange,** Manchester) and *A Streetcar Named Desire* **(Mercury Theatre,** Colchester). Television includes: *Any Human Heart; Law and Order UK; EastEnders; Casualty; Silent Witness; Fatal Passage; Coronation Street; Holby City; Extras; Love Soup; Taggart; Dance to the Music of Time* and *Midsomer Murders.* Film includes: *Messages;The Discovery of Heaven; Merchant Garcon;* and *The Wall of Tyranny.*

PATRICK DRIVER: Gordon

Theatre includes: *Bus Stop* **(New Vic** and **SJT)**; *Treasure Island* **(Watermill)**; *Faith Healer, Othello* and *Drowning on Dry Land* **(Salisbury Playhouse)**; *Anthropology* **(Latitude Festival)**; *Reverence* **(Southwark Playhouse)**; *Ma Rainey's Black Bottom, London Assurance,* and *Volpone* **(Royal Exchange,** Manchester)**;** *No, It Was You* **(Arcola Theatre)**; *Hunger, Imperfect Librarian, Theatre Dream, Half Machine, Icarus Falling* and *Poseidon* **(Primitive Science)**. As Joint Artistic Director of **Dialogue Productions,** he has appeared in: *Scorched* **(Old Vic Tunnels)**; *Wedding Day at The Cro-Magnons* **(Soho Theatre)**; *The Furies/Helter Skelter* **(Bush Theatre,** UK tour);*Top Dogs* **(Southwark Playhouse** and UK tour); *Merlin* **(Riverside Studios)**; *Heroes Like Us* **(Edinburgh Festival)**; *The M.C.* **(Edinburgh** and **Kilkenny Festivals,** UK, US and European tours)** and was A.D. on their production of *Monsieur Ibrahim* and *The Flowers of the Qur'an* **(Bush Theatre** Edinburgh and tour). Television includes: *Whistleblowers; Holby City; The Bill; The Office; The Last Chancers; Worst Week of My life; Peepshow; Grass; Doctors; People Like Us; My Hero; Ghosts* and *Mr Charity.*

PHILIP GLADWELL: Lighting Designer

Previously for **Pentabus**: *Origins and Kebab.* Other shows include: *Love The Sinner (National Theatre); Small Hours* **(Hampstead)**; *Miss Julie* **(Schaubuhne** Berlin); *Punk Rock* and *Mogadishu* **(Lyric Hammersmith/ *Tour*)**; 1984 and Macbeth **(Royal Exchange)**; *Oxford Street* **(Royal Court)**; *Five Guys Named Moe* **(Theatre Royal** Stratford/Edinburgh**)**; *The King And I* **(Curve** Leicester);*The Duchess of Malfi* **(Theatre Royal** Northampton); *Inheritance* and *Bodies* **(Live Theatre** Newcastle); *Testing The Echo* **(Out Of Joint)**; *Terminus* **(Abbey** and world tour); *Ghosts, The Member of the Wedding* and *Festa!* **(Young Vic)**; *The Fahrenheit Twins* **(Told By An Idiot)**; *Low Pay? Don't Pay!* **(Salisbury Playhouse)**; *I Ought To Be In Pictures* (**Library Theatre** Manchester); My Romantic History (**Bush, Traverse** – Fringe First); A Christmas Carol **(Dundee Rep)**; *Relatively Speaking, Daisy Pulls it off, Blithe Spirit* and *Black Comedy* **(Watermill)**; *Harvest* (UK Tour); *Melody* and *In the Bag* **(Traverse)**; *Mother Courage* **(Nottingham Playhouse/** UK tour); *Into the Woods* **(Derby Playhouse)**; *Bread & Butter* **(Tricycle)**; *After Dido* **(ENO)**; *Cosi Fan Tutte* **(WNO)**; *Rigoletto* and *La Wally* **(Holland Park)**; *Awakening* and *Another America: Fire* **(Sadler's Wells)**; *Il Trittico* **(Opera Zuid)** and *Falstaff* **(Grange Park)**

ANTHONY LAMBLE: Designer

Theatre includes: *Relatively Speaking* **(Watermill)**; *Twelfth Night* **(Ludlow Festival)**; *The Passing, The East Pier, Book-worms, The Comedy of Errors* and *The Playboy of the Western World* **(Abbey** Dublin); *Rum & Coca Cola* **(ETT / WYP/ Talawa)**; *Bedroom Farce* **(WYP)**; *Comedians* **(Lyric)**; *Loot* **(Tricycle)**; *Romeo and Juliet* **(Globe**/tour); *The English Game* **(Headlong)**; *The Entertainer* **(Old Vic)**; *Someone Who'll Watch Over Me* (West End); *The Price* (West End/**Tricycle**/tour); *The Caucasian Chalk Circle, Translations, Sing Yer Heart Out for the Lads, A Midsummer Night's Dream,* and *As You Like It* **(National)** and numerous productions for the **RSC, Royal Court, Menier, OSC, Bush, Chichester, Sheffield, Shared Experience (Belgrade)** and the film *The Secret Audience.* Dance and opera credits include: *Facing Viv* **(ENB)**; *L'Orfeo* (Tokyo); *Palace in the Sky* **(ENO)** and *Broken Fiction* **(ROH)**.

ORLA O'LOUGHLIN: Director

Orla O'Loughlin joined Pentabus Theatre in 2007, moving from the **Royal Court Theatre** where she was the International Associate. Directing work includes: *Tales of the Country* (National Tour); *Origins* **(Pleasance/Theatre Severn)**; *Blithe Spirit, Black Comedy* and *Relatively Speaking* **(Watermill Theatre)**; *Kebab* **(Dublin International Festival, Royal Court Theatre)**; *How Much is your Iron?* **(Young Vic)**; *The Hound of the Baskervilles* **(West Yorkshire Playhouse/**National Tour/ West End); *Small Talk: Big Picture* **(BBC World Service/ ICA/ Royal Court Theatre)**; *Lorca the Poet; Lorca the Playwright* **(National Theatre)**; *A Dulditch Angel* (National Tour); *The Fire Raisers, Sob Stories and Refrain* **(BAC)** and two large scale site specific projects: *Shuffle* **(National Youth Theatre,** Merry Hill Shopping Centre) and *Underland* (200 feet below ground at Clearwell Caves). Orla was winner of the James Menzies Kitchin Directors Award and recipient of the Carlton Bursary at the **Donmar Warehouse.**

TIM PRICE: Writer

Tim Price's plays include: *Will and George*, shortlisted for the Verity Bargate Award 2011; *Salt Root and Roe* **(Donmar Warehouse)** to premiere at **Trafalgar Studios** in November 2011). In 2012 his play *The Radicalisation of Bradley Manning* will open for **National Theatre Wales** in Haverfordwest. His musical, *Café Cariad*, was staged by the **National Youth Theatre of Wales** in 2007. He has written short plays for **The Royal Court, Soho Theatre, Paines Plough, Sherman Cymru, Theatre 503, Nabokov** and **Drywrite**. For television he has written for *Holby City, Casualty, EastEnders, Secret Diary of a Call Girl, The New Worst Witch, Sold*, and his own Welsh language gangster drama *Y Pris*, for which he won a Celtic Drama Festival Award, and was nominated for a Bafta **Cymru** and a **Prix Europa**. He co-runs a new writing theatre company in Cardiff called **Dirty Protest**, with nights based in a Mongolian Yurt in Cardiff.

CHRISTOPHER SHUTT: Sound Designer
Previously for **Pentabus**: *Origins. War Horse, White Guard, Burnt by the Sun, Every Good Boy Deserves Favour, Coram Boy, Humble Boy, Not About Nightingales* and *Machinal* **(National Theatre)**; *Disappearing Number, Elephant Vanishes, Mnemonic, Street of Crocodiles* and *Three Lives of Lucie Cabrol* **(Complicite)**; *Piaf, Hecuba* and *Man Who Had All The Luck* **(Donmar)**; *Ruined* and *Judgment Day* **(Almeida)**; *Aunt Dan* and *Lemon, Serious Money* and *Road* **(Royal Court)**; *Far Away* **(Bristol)**; *All My Sons* and *Arturo Ui* **(Broadway)**; *The Bacchae* and *Little Otik* **(National Theatre of Scotland)** *Moon for the Misbegotten* and *All About My Mother* **(Old Vic)**; *King Lear, Much Ado, King John* and *Romeo and Juliet* **(RSC)**; *Julius Caesar* and *School for Scandal* **(Barbican)**; *Beyond the Horizon/Spring Storm* **(Northampton and The National)**. Radio: *Shropshire Lad, Tennyson's Maud, Disappearing Number*. 2 Drama Desk Awards. Olivier Nominations: *War Horse, Coram Boy, Piaf, EGBDF*. Tony Award: *War Horse*.

JONATHAN SMITH: Sid
Jonathan trained at LAMDA 2007/10 during which time he performed in: *A Time to Keep; The Duchess of Malfi; Guys and Dolls; Nabokov's Gloves* and *The York Realist*. Recent theatre includes *State of Nature* **(Theatrescience)** at the **Eden Project**.

BEN WEBB: Assistant Director
As Writer & Director: So Little of You Left **(People Show Studios** and Tour**)**; *His Spread Legs* **(Tara Arts Studio** and Tour**)**; *The Actor Has Told of His Pain* (forthcoming). As Director: *A Polar Bear Play* – devised **(Old Red Lion, Green Man Festival** and **Shunt)**; *The Bath House* **(Squat Collective)**; *Notes for First Time Astronauts, Gypsy Girl, Give Generously* **(Soho Theatre)**; *Godfather Death* **(Wimbledon Theatre** and **Brighton Festival)**; *The Kathy Acker Mobile Library* **(Poetry Café)**; *Und* by Howard Barker **(Canal Café)**; *Less* **(King's Head)**; *The Taming of the Shrew* **(British Touring Shakespeare)**. As Assistant Director: *Orphans* **Paines Plough, Traverse Theatre, Birmingham Rep,** and **Soho Theatre)**.

PENTABUS THEATRE

Pentabus Theatre believes in asking questions and telling stories that resonate with audiences locally, nationally and internationally.

At the heart of this work is our rural location which affords us a unique perspective on, and relationship to, the world.

Our mission is to pioneer engaging, provocative and surprising new work that connects people and places.

The Pentabus Experiment or Concept as it was originally known was formed in 1973. The company originally toured new work to the five counties in the West Midlands. Productions during those early years played in a wide variety of venues including village halls, schools, pubs and numerous outdoor locations. As time went on the company extended its reach to include national and international projects and began eliciting the attention of national press and collecting awards.

Pentabus Theatre continues to pioneer new work. Recent productions include the acclaimed *Origins* about the early life of Charles Darwin, made in association with Blind Summit puppetry company, South Bank Show Award shortlisted *White Open Spaces*, a series of monologues about race and belonging in the countryside **(Soho Theatre, BBC Radio 4)**, *Kebab* by Romanian writer Gianina Carbunariu **(Royal Court, Dublin International Festival)** and two ground-breaking, large-scale site-specific projects: *Underland,* which took place in a series of underground caverns at Clearwell Caves in the Forest of Dean and *Shuffle* with the **National Youth Theatre**, which, with a cast of over 60, played to an audience of thousands at Merry Hill, one of the UK's largest out of town shopping centres.

'The excellent Pentabus' Guardian

TIME OUT April 2010:

'You never know where a Pentabus production might pop up. It might be on stage at the Royal Court or Dublin International Festival – but it could just as easily be in a village hall or even a cave 200 feet underground. The Ludlow-based company has recently celebrated its 35th birthday – and with it, a history of making eclectic and innovative work that, while firmly rooted in the soil of its rural locale, branches out to embrace issues of national significance.'

WRITERS WEEKS

Our annual writers weeks have become a key element of what we do. During these weeks we invite writers to come and explore a local issue with us. These have found us, amongst other things, out in the wilds following a fox hunt, witnessing life in an abattoir and working shifts in a Michelin-starred kitchen. These weeks have led to a number of exciting commissions and projects including *Pigs*, a series of ten minute plays inspired by the Slow Food Movement which premiered at the **Edinburgh Festival** and *The Hunting Season* where writers, allowed unprecedented access to the local hunt, asked just what it is about this centuries old tradition that continues to drive such a wedge between town and country. This year we focused on the annual *May Fair* where in a tradition that reaches back hundreds of years our sleepy market town is transformed into a bustling and frenetic fairground. The result *May Fair* written by John Donnelly, Gbolahan Obisesan, Joe Harbot, Lou Ramsden and Vanessa Oakes will premiere at **Latitude Festival** this July.

'I like the Pentabus policy - village halls as important as theatres. Finding new ways to bring stories and plays to people. **Michael Palin**

HAMPSTEAD THEATRE is one of the U.K.'s leading new writing companies. Throughout its long history, the Theatre has supported a thriving local, national and international playwriting culture. We commission plays in order to enrich and enliven this culture. We support, develop and produce the work of new writers, emerging writers, established writers, mid-career writers and senior writers and have a proud tradition for creating the conditions for their plays and careers to develop.

The list of playwrights who had their early work produced at Hampstead Theatre and who are now filling theatres all over the country and beyond include Mike Leigh, Michael Frayn, Brian Friel, Terry Johnson, Hanif Kureishi, Simon Block, Abi Morgan, Rona Munro, Tamsin Oglesby, Harold Pinter, Shelagh Stephenson, debbie tucker green, Crispin Whittell, Roy Williams and Dennis Kelly.

In January 2010, Edward Hall was appointed Artistic Director of Hampstead Theatre. His inaugural season was a box office success culminating in two West End transfers: Mike Leigh's *Ecstasy* (Duchess Theatre) and the Hampstead Downstairs production *Belongings* (Trafalgar Studios 2).

Hampstead Downstairs seats 98 and stages raw, edgy and experimental work. The audience decide for themselves what they think of the work, with their decisions not being predetermined by media reviews. Since its opening in November 2010, previous productions include small hours directed by Katie Mitchell, *.45* written by Gary Lennon and *The Stock Da'wa* directed by Kathy Burke

HAMPSTEAD THEATRE'S new autumn and spring season 2011/2012 will continue to delight, inspire and engage with such directors as Katie Mitchell, Richard Eyre and Roger Michell taking to the stage.

Hampstead Theatre, Eton Avenue, Swiss Cottage,

London, NW3 3EU

www.hampsteadtheatre.com

FOR ONCE TOUR 2012

In Spring 2012, For Once will embark on a national tour in association with Sherman Cymru, commencing with a week at their venue in Cardiff. Full details will be posted on the companies' websites:

www.pentabus.co.uk
www.shermancymru.co.uk

SHERMAN CYMRU

SHERMAN CYMRU aims to make and present great theatre that is ambitious, inventive and memorable for its audiences, and to create strong, responsive and enriching relationships with its communities. The company produce work in both English and Welsh, and tour widely within Wales and the UK.

Cyngor Celfyddydau Cymru
Arts Council of Wales

Noddir gan
Lywodraeth Cymru
Sponsored by
Welsh Government

CARDIFF
CAERDYDD

Writer's Acknowledgments:

Orla O'Loughlin, Kate Budgen, Ben Webb, and all at Pentabus and Hampstead theatres respectively; Nicky Lund, Charlotte Loveridge, Scott Arthur, Martin Taylor Smith, Sally Newman Kidd, Penny Dunachie, Mark Jefferies, Joel Horwood, Vicky Fletcher-Gilhuys, Camilla Harrison, Phil Mayall, Tamsin Osler, Phil Johnstone, Will Holland and the La Bécasse brothers, The Church Inn, Vaughans, Harry Hepple, Chloë Moss, James Graham, Roger Williams, Paul Rees, Phil and Menna Price, Matt, Maryline, Gary Marsh and Sophia Price.

N.B. This script went to print before the opening night and may therefore differ slightly to the performed version.

FOREWORD

In 2009 Pentabus Theatre became members of **Slow Food**: a movement that boasts 85,000 members in 132 countries and states that gastronomy is indissolubly tied to politics, agriculture and the environment. Inspired by these concerns, and the fact that at the time the **UK Slow Food** head office was based in Ludlow, we hosted a writers' week meeting with campaigners, farmers, butchers, retailers, consumers and chefs to see what stories might emerge. The direct result of the week was *Pigs* a series of short plays by Abbie Spallen, Alan Pollock, Deborah McAndrew, Nicola Jones and Tim Price that premiered at the Edinburgh Festival later that year. Tim's piece, a monologue from the perspective of a 17 year-old boy, was the beginning of *For Once*.

Whilst in Ludlow Tim spent a lot of time, as he describes, 'wandering aimlessly around'. These wanderings led him, amongst other places, to the youth centre. During conversations with the young people there, he found their relationship to the town's foodie reputation was stated with indifference, bemusement or hostility. It became clear they didn't feel invited to the table. His further wanderings led him to the local college where he was surprised by a prominent notice board covered in anti-speeding slogans, teen death statistics and young drivers' courses. These shaped Tim's thinking about the role of young people in the town and became the genesis of Sid's story involving the all too imaginable tragedy at the heart of *For Once*.

I'd like to thank Tim for his unswerving commitment to this play and our first production of it. His insight, tenacity and good humour have been an inspiration to those he has worked with and a fitting tribute to his subject.

Orla O'Loughlin

Tim Price

For Once

In memory of
Martin Rutter

Characters

Sid, *17, sporty, possibly wearing a beenie. Blind in one eye.*
April, *45, schoolteacher, prides herself on her youthfulness.*
Gordon, *46, tendency to dishevel, big man about town.*

(/) indicates when the next line should be spoken.

Scene One

A country kitchen.

The characters occupy the same space but are not aware of each other. It is as if they are in the same place but at different times. **April** *irons and folds shirts, and does the washing up.* **Gordon** *is on hold on a mobile, going through insurance documents and eating.* **Sid** *is mainly concerned with his laptop, mobile and walking around.*

April I look at him. I look at the dog. I look at him.

Beat.

Even the dog is embarrassed. I throw myself at the dog, I'm not a doggy person, but I feel sorry for him. And probably, a bit sorry for myself. So I crawl across the floor towards the dog.

Eventually Sid joins us and we make some progress. I watch Sid pat his head and I think; this *isn't* how the books said it would be . . .

A little bottle of eye drops rolls out of Sid's pocket and I reach for them but Sid gets there first. I'm glad the dog's there, because I think I might cry.

Sid Can I go now?

Gordon Take the dog with you.

April *claps her hands excitedly, before stopping, embarrassed at* **Sid***'s underwhelm.*

April Gordon sits on the sofa but I can't bring myself to sit down.

April *swings her arms not sure what to do with herself.*

Gordon That went well?

April I stop myself from smacking him on the head with the dog bowl, and give him a look instead.

Gordon He's never liked dogs.

April   Why the hell did we buy him one then?

He takes his glasses off and starts cleaning them with his tie.

Gordon   All I know is, that boy is making faster progress than you want him to. It's time we just . . . got on with our lives.

April   I want to answer, but I seize up. It's hard to imagine, but there's something about the way he sits on the sofa, cleaning his glasses, it's very threatening.

Gordon   We're on track! We are on track.

Beat.

Small steps. Small victories. Taking each day as it comes. Times like these you discover a lot about yourself, family and friends. And this place, it's not a town; it's a village with attitude.

Beat.

The cards, you can see for yourself, been a great comfort. I come down here quite a lot at night, read them all. Remind myself.

Gordon *reads a card.*

This one's from my cousin. He runs a prison. One of the biggest in the country, Sunderland way.

Beat.

Very interesting fellow. He says when they fight, when the prisoners fight, they take privileges away from them; gym, library, all that. But when they've got less to do, they fight more, so really if they fight, they need more privileges. If that's what you're there for, to stop them fighting, give them stuff to do.

Beat.

That's what I'm like I think. Except I don't fight, I get familiar, take things for granted. Something like this pulls everything into focus.

Beat.

Things have never been so clear. April and I, some of our happiest times together have been in a crisis!

Beat.

Like when Sid swallowed a whistle! Thought he was going to die, put the fear of God up us, rushed him to the hospital, by the time we got there we were doubled up trying not to laugh; every time he breathed he . . .

Whistles a breath.

My boy.

Beat.

No, April and I, I think we're one of those couples, like the prisoners, get too familiar, and then something happens and by God we're glad we're there for each other. She is a blessing.

Gordon *reads another card.*

Mark Trott.

Whenever **Gordon** *says* 'Mark Trott' *he always points in the same direction.*

Runs the deli, he told me, he and his wife, once a fortnight, take a bath together.

Gordon *reacts.*

I know for a fact he's on a water meter. And they've split up now, so what does that say?

Beat.

April and I have never gone in for that sort of thing thank you very much. We have a much more . . .

Beat.

Civilised relationship. Even now. There's been no histrionics.

Gordon *closes a card.*

Sid   I'm on Facebook for the first time in ages and trying to put the drops in my eye and it's going everywhere.

It feels like I'm plugging back into the Matrix after I've swallowed the red pill. Everything is fake now; only I haven't got any special powers to help me get through a conversation.

Luke, Owen and Alex are all offline.

Pause.

The webcam comes on and I see me but I'm all pixelated. Like in a film. I'm trying to fix it when:

April   SID? SID?

Sid   I wait for it.

April   SIDNEY?

Sid   There it is. The full name that she gave me.

April   Can you come down here please?

Sid   I love my Mum. I do. I love her. I'd do anything for her. If she asked me to lift a car up with my bare hands I'd find the strength to do it. I'd like it if she asked me that. But she never asks for stuff like that.

Beat.

I go down to the lounge and I try really hard not to be a prick. But she starts talking and it's the same stuff it always is and I find myself making the least amount of noise possible. I'm embarrassed for her.

April   We've got something for you.

Sid   And in the middle of the room is a black lab. It's not a puppy it's a proper dog.

April   It's yours.

Sid   It just sits there.

Beat.

I feel sorry for him. Mum tries to call him over and it takes ages.

April *makes all sorts of encouraging noises – underscore.*

Sid *is uncomfortable with* **April***'s persistence.*

Sid   She'll get there in the end.

Beat.

Mum won't give up until she's found me a new friend.

Beat.

Gordon   Get up off the sofa and stroke the dog Sid.

Sid   I get down and Mum joins me, she gives me some biscuits to give him and we kneel close and pat him.

Gordon   What are we going to call him?

Sid   Neil.

April   Neil?

Sid   Don't ask me why.

I can tell she hates it. I see them catch each other's eyes over the dog. It was a look I haven't seen since we played Monopoly when I was a kid. One of them would catch the other cheating. Cheating so I'd win, you know, forgetting to charge me rent or whatever. Mum saw Dad cheating again, and the dog was called Neil. Dad introduces himself to the dog as if they're on some committee.

Gordon   Hello Neil. I'm Gordon, Walker.

Beat.

Sid   Later on Mum shows me a dog-gate in the utility room. I look back at Neil in his square of the world and he seems utterly pointless.

Gordon   That night April was off to some concert, I'm off doing my own thing and Sid well, he was too, bless him. That's how our family works.

Beat.

We might be in the kitchen, I'll be listening to the radio, Sid'll have his iPod on and April will be watching some foreign film on her laptop, but we'll still be together, we just gravitate towards each other.

Beat.

I used to quite like flat hunting, in nearby towns, I wouldn't buy or rent any or anything, I just liked keeping my toe in the property market. I went as far as Bath once to look at a flat. It's a lot like this place. Small size, big mouth!

Beat.

This flat, I walk around, and the living room has these little French doors, and they look out over the town. Stacey, the agent, opens the doors for me and we stand looking out together. There isn't a street I recognise, or a shop I know. I could be anywhere in the world. Before I know it, I'm haggling with her and I haven't even seen the bathroom! All on a blast of fresh air.

Beat.

I get her down to one eight five, and it's a bit embarrassing, because I can see she's ready to put it to the vendor. I can't buy it but I'm dying to hear what they'll say, I want them to say yes, just to teach me a lesson, like when you feel a pain in your chest and you want it to be a mild heart attack so you'll finally stop eating cheese.

*

Sid I'm at the fridge and Mum starts hugging me and crying. She's saying lots of stuff that I can't listen to but I know the rhythms. I don't know what to do to stop it. It's all I can do to hold her these days.

Um. When she hugs me. It's like she's celebrating? It's not her fault. I try so hard to put up with it, but it makes me nervous,

'I get nervous when she starts crying.'

Gordon It's the whole fight or flight thing.

Sid I don't want to fight or run away from Mum.

Even when she's chirpy and says things like:

April (*chirpy*) Both drops before you go to bed now.

Sid Whenever her voice wobbles Dad never ever looks at her, he looks straight at me as if he wants his stony face to take the place of her voice. Her voice wobbles because when she sees me, she sees the ghosts.

Beat.

Everyone saw the ghosts when they were alive. 'Where's the other two?' Me and Luke would get if uh, Owen and Alex were doing art. Getting our names mixed up, giving us crap nicknames like the four stooges.

Everyone knows which one I am now.

Beat.

I go round Luke's. His Dad's on the council; runs a cheese festival. Luke used to call him the Big Cheese, we all did. Mrs Reeves hugs me but she's so small it's awkward; her head comes up to about there. We used to call her 'Travel Mum' – does the same job as a real Mum just more compact.

Sid *manages a brief smile.*

The Big Cheese shakes my hand, which puts me in some kind of groove. They're pleased at how sociable I am. So I start using their names mid-sentence:

'Well you say that, *Mr Reeves*, but if you dwell on things too much, it'll take over your life!'

'Thank you *Mrs Reeves*, I will have a cup of tea.'

And on and on I go and I feel like I should be in fancy dress. I'm like a gap-year son believing his own lies that he never got lonely. And it hits me. Perhaps this is what everyone else does? Perhaps this is what adults do? I can just act happy. Perhaps I can do this with Mum?

April   I decide to get out of the house and go to Tesco's when I bump into Ronnie Trott. Ronnie's one of those women who wears wooden jewellery, swims in the river, that sort of thing? Immediately she starts over-sharing about Mark running off with the estate agent. Hence the pathetic basket.

She's telling me Tesco's is a designated 'red zone' because 'anything can happen' and I feel myself gripping a can of hairspray. All I can think of is Sid walking out of the room without turning back, and here Ronnie is wallowing in her misery: 'The Globe, the Buttery, I can't go anywhere, it's a bloody land-grab April' and before I know it, I've squirted her in the eye with the hairspray.

'Jesus April!'

'The seal's broken the seal was broke!'

I try showing her but she can't see because . . . I've squirted her eyes with hairspray.

'Dean!'

I taught Dean art, he works here part-time.

'The seal was broken.'

Dean takes us to a staff toilet, where we watch Ronnie wash her eyes and I try to kill myself from inside. She's going to have a field day, plus she's probably allergic. Everything needs to be organic and reared in a stable relationship. I look around the room and for some reason I turn to Dean and say:

'So, what goes on in here then?'

'This is where people come to piss. Sometimes a dump. Depends.'

(**April** *winces with regret.*)

'Thank you! Dean. I get the picture. I thought this might be where you come to avoid work. It doesn't matter.'

Ronnie washes her eyes and makes little noises.

'There's an offer on oven trays,' says Dean.

April *breathes deeply.*

I look at him. And I look at Ronnie.

It strikes me that I probably hate her.

Gordon Treasurer for the Cider Festival, Friend of the Castle, Vice-president of the football club, Town Hall Committee, Twinning Association Committee, Bread Walk Campaign Steering Committee, that one hasn't got a leader, *as such*, but it's probably me, and there are a couple of others I can't remember now.

Beat.

But the point is it's very hard to be a professional in this town and not be lasso-ed into running things. If this country goes to war again, they should run the war effort out of the castle, it'll be over in weeks I promise you. April and I were in town once, and we get stopped for the umpteenth time, outside the butchers.

April Is there anyone you won't talk to?

Gordon And I can't think of anyone.

Just because I don't collect grudges and vendettas for a hobby like her, she thinks I'm the one with the problem! I'm not the one who drives to Craven Arms for a prescription, because I've fallen out with the chemist. It has its benefits being the way April is – don't get me wrong, you don't want to get on the wrong side of her, that's for sure.

Beat.

When we were first married, we had dinner with a couple of my work colleagues; I think it was a works thing? And one of the fellahs, James, dead now, calls me 'Flash Gordon'.

April   'What do you call him?'

April *holds a passive aggressive smile.*

Gordon   Everyone shifts uncomfortably, because she's smiling, but with a sort of, *purpose.* If you get what I mean? 'It's a bit of joke we have in the office. His clothes are a bit boring that's all,' says James.

Gordon *smiles and then shudders at the memory.*

I don't know where to look, James's wife looks at me, and April keeps smiling straight at him. She was relentless, she didn't stop until he turned bright red. She'd let him be loud and crass all night but when he displeased her, she was like Darth Vader! She humiliates him to a biological degree and then she turns to me and says:

April (*sweetly*)   Will you share a dessert with me darling?

Gordon *shudders.*

Gordon   I still wake up sweating about it.

There's a lovely network here, I don't miss Birmingham. Lots of people in town, once a month they'll go to London, or Birmingham every other weekend. I never feel the need. And the last time I went to Birmingham I was in a bar, and I went to the toilet and when I pulled my trousers up, some bugger had swiped my wallet out of the pocket. Under the –

Makes action.

Here. It's doors open all hours. Took a bit of getting used to, it was important to April we bring Sid up in the country, like she was. We hadn't been here long and I was in the Blue Boar one night and a young farmer was drinking there. Got chatting, young fellah, but old, like farmers are. Like talking to a fossil.

Beat.

'Everyone here knows everyone else's business.'

He doesn't even look at me he just says, 'If everyone knew everyone else's business, no one would live here. Specially the buggers from off!' I wrote it off as just a bit of friendly local hostility but now I think he was on to something.

April   Caught Sid with a bong once. He was on his way to a party; you can't call them barn dances, even though they're dancing, in a barn. It's a party. They were on their way to a party, and they were walking through town, the four of them. I was on my way to a meeting at the Assembly Rooms to see how we could get more young people to use the facility, and this lot were trying to persuade adults to buy them booze from the Spar.

I read an article about these drones in Afghanistan, how they find their direction not by satellite geo-positioning or anything, but by their distance from each other. That's how these four walked, if you watched them. Utterly, bloody directionless; but never more than two or three feet away from each other.

I see Sid, lolling behind.

'Sid!'

He turns, sees me, takes a bag off his shoulder and passes it to Luke before walking towards me. It's about as subtle as shouting 'I've got something in here and you're not gonna like it!'

With my best I'm-in-charge-of-the-yard tone I demand the bag from Luke. Usually he would have attempted charming his way out of it but I realise now he was far too stoned, and he hands it over.

Sid (*gritted teeth*)   Why are you trying to make me look like an idiot?

April   I'm not.

Sid   You're embarrassing me.

April   You're being ridiculous.

Sid   Mum, please.

April *holds something up to represent the bong.*

April   What's this?

Sid *shuffles his weight and looks at his shoes.*

April   Sid?

Sid   That? That's a . . .

April   What?

Sid   It's a . . .

April   What is it?

Sid   Well um . . .

April   Sid?

Sid   Bunsen burner. It's a Bunsen burner. Yeah.

April *looks at it in disbelief.*

April   As I try to look Sid in the eye I hear a very faint giggle from one of the other three. I look at Owen who judders as he tries not to laugh. Alex bites his fist and Luke turns his back to me to let out a giggle.

Sid Science project.

April If this is what you do in science Sid, what the hell are you smoking at the weekends?

And the three of them step away and howl with laughter, clutching their tummies.

I look at Sid, unimpressed, but a smile creeps across his face and before I know it, I'm giggling as well.

'Bunsen burner!' shouts Alex and he goes down on his knees. Luke and Owen wipe tears from their eyes and have to lean on each other, Sid's caught between them and me, but he can't help it, I can't help it . . .

Sid *cracks up.*

April *cracks up.*

I've *never* seen them like this! It's so contagious, like watching babies laugh, and I can't stop myself . . .

April *laughs.*

It's like I'm part of the gang. Before long, we're all crying with laughter and I think

April *tries to compose herself, perhaps wipes tears.*

Seeing me laughing makes them laugh even more which makes me laugh more and

April *laughs.*

I think I'm going to wet myself! And I'm holding a bong in the middle of town!

April *tries to compose herself.*

'I'd better put this away,' I say.

April *laughs.*

And that is it! They all hit the floor, now they *are* like four big babies, holding their tummies rolling around my feet and I can't

April *laughs.*

Do anything with them!

April *laughs and gathers herself together.*

Finally, everybody calms down just long enough so they can get to their feet.

Beat.

They're still incapable of saying anything without descending into a giggling fit and there's a moment where we all look at each other and none of us can remember what we're doing. Alex says 'Party?' And they all sort of take their leave of me.

April   So you're off then are you?

Sid   Uh yeah. Yeah. Okay.

April   They start to drift.

'I'll take this with me.'

April *raises the bong.*

They just about manage a . . .

April *gives two thumbs up.*

Pause.

Sid resists the directionless pull just long enough to run back and hug me.

Beat.

In the middle of town.

Beat.

In front of all his friends.

April *gives two thumbs up.*

Gordon   There are things that will drive you a bit mad about this place.

Beat.

You will get to know everyone over time.

Beat.

But everyone in this town goes to other places all the time
as well, so you can't go anywhere without bumping into
someone you know. We went to Corsica. Who sits next to us
in a restaurant?

Gordon *points to Mark Trott's deli.*

Mark Trott's daughter.

Beat.

Go to Hay, Kiddie, Gloucester, someone will shout your
name out. I was in a lay-by outside Keele, a lay-by, not a
main thoroughfare, and I've got Dave Grimshaw tapping
on the window telling me my driver-side brake light isn't
working. Sid hates it, he's always complaining,

Sid (*underscore*)   Why don't we live in a city?/ Or a town?
Or a village near a town or a city, that would be alright,
somewhere next to somewhere interesting. I'm not asking
much.

Gordon   But he's only complaining because he can't get
away with the stuff he wants to. Underage drinking, pot
smoking, anything he shouldn't be doing, there's eyes
everywhere. I told him:

'The more people who know you, the more you've got to be
whiter than white. Keep up appearances.'

Beat.

That's why sometimes I book myself a little holiday and don't
tell anyone. Not even April. I tell her I've got some work
conference, Wednesday and Thursday night somewhere,
and I go and book myself in somewhere for a couple of
nights. Still go to work, but I go and sleep in the hotel or
B&B, just to have a break. Get to know a new little area, a
new little town, bit of peace and quiet, and get on with my

own thing. I've stayed all over the Midlands, once every couple of weeks I'd have a night somewhere, just to have a little break. Plus it's nice to meet people who don't know you.

One night I was staying in Birmingham for a night or two. Just to have a break. Went into a trendy bar, loud music. All the time I'm thinking why have I come here? I could go to the Feathers and plonk myself at the bar and speak to anyone who comes through the door. Why come here when I don't know anyone?

Beat.

I order a lager and it comes with a piece of lime in the neck which I can't get out. I try sitting at the bar, but the stools are so high, I can't get comfy so I go and sit in the corner and wish I'd bought a newspaper because the magazines there aren't my kind of thing. That's what I love doing more than anything, a pint and a newspaper. Every bloke I know starts the newspaper from the back. I don't know why they don't put the sport on the front and news at the back? I was thinking, if I get chatting to someone, that's what I'll go on. Why isn't there a newspaper with sport on the front? I had my drink, and my corner, and my conversation ready. A couple of other guys over the other side of the room, they'd left their lime in the neck. So I left mine in too.

I spend about fifteen, twenty minutes, thinking about what I should do, and I think perhaps I should pop out and get a newspaper, so I've got something to do, so it doesn't look like anything. But then this young chap comes in with the side of his head shaved. He's got working boots on and tight jeans and I think, perhaps he might like a newspaper too? He's on his own. He might like something to read, and I'm going out. Seems daft.

He orders a drink and starts chatting to the barman. They look like they know each other, so I pick my drink up and I walk over to the bar and I'm trying to think, how are we going to sort this newspaper money situation out, I could just buy them I suppose?

'Alright mate?' he says.

I open my mouth but I'm not sure what to say.

'Just, you keep staring.'

Gordon *is speechless.*

Sid   Travel Mum and the Big Cheese are weirdly excited and crying now and again. I put Neil in their kitchen and I realise, not many young people have been round much. I don't mind them dragging it out but I don't have much to say. After a while, they tell me to go upstairs. On the way up, I step past a picture of Luke stroking a dolphin and I think, that dolphin's alive and Luke's dead.

Beat.

It catches me like when a bouncy ball hits you on the ear in the schoolyard? Travel Mum puts her hand on my back. She pats me. Everyone's touching everyone these days, it's weird. Like I patted Neil not because I wanted to but because I knew I should. I didn't want to pat him; I don't want her patting me.

Beat.

Luke's room is bigger than mine. It's still a mess.

'Take anything you want. Clothes, games, anything. I'd rather you have it than charity.' The Big Cheese stays by the door eating a biscuit. I start to say something about not wanting anything, but the Big Cheese won't hear of it. 'Luke would have wanted you to have something. We want you to have something.' And he winks, which makes me want to run through the wall like in the cartoons leaving a Sid-shaped hole.

I fiddle with his hifi.

He was the only boy in college to prefer CDs to MP3. He was the only one who could afford them.

'It's lovely seeing you in this room again Sid,' she says and she shrugged.

Pause.

You either have nothing in common with your mate's parents or everything.

Beat.

With that shrug I realise she's just as awkward and confused about all this as me.

I decide to tell Travel Mum about the time Luke rang me from France just to tell me he was happy. That's all he had to say. She'd want to hear about that phone call. What she didn't want to hear was what was now coming out of the stereo.

'Shut the Fuck Up' by STFU blares from the hifi. **Sid** *hangs his head in shame as the music plays for five–ten seconds.*

The music stops.

'I'll leave you to it,' she says.

Even from beyond the grave Luke was still making me look like a prick.

Gordon   I used to be an insurance rep, livestock and farming equipment, but I'm more desk-bound now. I still try to get out on the road once in a while. Keep my hand in.

Beat.

Reps have a great life – the open road, no office politics, no irritating colleagues. It can get a bit lonely, but quite often you'll hit it off with other reps as you pass through, you've got so much in common.

Beat.

I'm at the bar having a drink.

'Andrew?'

But he doesn't hear me, and he heads into the restaurant. I thought I should probably let him have his dinner and I'll catch up with him later. But before I know it I'm standing at his table.

'Mind if I join you?'

Beat.

He has steak, I have scampi. We talk, I can't really remember what about, I think it was just work stuff, so that's fine.

Beat.

We finish dinner and he starts going on about emails he's got to send, and I'm in the middle of preparing some quotes for a new client, but when the waiter clears our plates I think sod it, and order another round of drinks. He rolls his eyes: 'We've been here before!'

Beat.

His room is massive. His firm books executive rooms and the difference is immense. Double sinks, broadband, mini-bar, it's big enough to just be called 'a bar'. We give that a bit of a hammering and by the end we're both a little 'tired and emotional' shall we say.

I wind him up about his pants. He's got boxes of pants stacked everywhere. Pants. In. Boxes. I open box after box, all different colours and styles.

'Oi Del Boy, you got some kind of dodgy deal going on?'

But apparently his expenses cover 'sundries'. I take a box and open them while he fixes some G and T's. 'Sloggies'. I look at them and can't help thinking how new they look compared to my pants. I don't think mine even come in boxes?

'April buys my pants.'

I'm so excited about his expenses, he shows me what else he can get; CDs, cinema tickets, underwear, clothes . . . you name it he claims it.

'I can't believe all this,' I say looking at the stuff on the bed. And then I can't really remember what happened.

Long pause.

But I remember he insisted I take something, a CD or a pair of pants. I didn't want anything but he was so insistent. He said, 'I'm not letting you go until you take something.'

(*Reflective.*) Can't even remember what I took now.

Sid   In Luke's room, I catch myself in his mirror. It's warped in the heat and I look stretched between two worlds.

I curl up and think about the time we stopped speaking, and I used to see him around town. I think about how he was the only friend who sent postcards. I think about all the places I'm never going to see his handwriting on the back of.

Beat.

Mr Reeves insists on driving me and Neil home.

What no one tells you about having one eye is that it gets tired really easy. I was trying not to fall asleep when I realised he'd stopped. He turned to me and said, 'I want to set up an anti-speeding foundation in memory of Luke, Owen and Alex.' I feel my eye going to sleep. I try to fight it, but the car is really warm. I go for long blinks. When I close my eye, another me slips into Costa coffee,

(*Quickly.*) Owen shouts at the manager, it's turned nasty, I don't know if I should step in, I channel adrenaline, while everyone looks at us, like we're scum.

(*Slow.*) 'Are you okay Sid?' The Big Cheese is looking at me.

'You look a bit pale,' he says. I tell him I'm fine, and concentrate on one of his eyes. He starts again, and it's only moments when my eye goes.

(*Quicker.*) 'Why don't you call the police? What are you gonna say? Excuse me officer these fuckers here aren't buying enough drinks,' says Luke. I laugh. I laugh because he said 'fuckers'. He doesn't care about winning the argument; he just wants to offend people. Luke sweeps the coffee off the table, next to us, I win bowling.

(*Slow.*) 'I want you to be the face of the foundation, as the only survivor of the crash.'

The crash.

Owen does his Velociraptor and we're laughing so much it turns us upside down. My foot kicks the back window out and my phone won't ring Mum because I haven't got any signal.

(*Long pause.*)

'I don't remember anything from that day.' He smiles, as if he understands. Sitting next to him on the way home makes me feel like somehow I've cheated the boys but I don't know how. Just as I get out he can't stop himself saying:

'The council want you Sid. I can't raise the money without you attached.' I look at him the way Neil must have when my Mum turned up to get him. What can I do in your world?

April   I'm still reeling from the hairspray incident when I drive home and see Sid walking along one of the lanes with Neil. I pull over to give him a lift.

Sid   I don't want a lift, I want to walk. Need the fresh air.

April   So I roll alongside him for a few yards with the window down. I tell him about Ronnie and play up Dean's role. Lately, I tend to overplay any teen interaction I have.

'Do you think you'd like to move away now? We could move away if you want?'

He shakes his head and keeps walking.

But I'm determined not to let him out of my sight. I roll alongside him calling his name, telling him, I'm not going to let this drop when . . .

April *strikes something to create a loud bang!*

I don't know what happened but I'm covered in white powder and my face hurts.

Sid   Mum? Mum? Are you okay? The airbag's gone off.

April   I get out and realise I've rolled into the back of a parked car. I feel like I've been punched. Sid and Neil look at me like I'm the biggest bloody idiot they've ever seen. Their pity jolts me into action more than anything else.

We get back in the car and put Neil on the backseat. I drive home in silence.

As I pull the shopping out, Gordon joins us. Sid tries to explain, but I cut him off. I don't want Gordon involved and besides, I think the airbag flicked a switch in me.

Gordon   The May fair comes to town.

Beat.

I can't park near the house so I'm a little later getting in.

Beat.

April is in the shower, singing 'At Last' by Etta James.

Underscore: **April** *humming 'At last'.*

I unpack my overnight bag but I can't concentrate. I find myself sitting on the edge of the bed listening. She used to sing all the time when we first got together. Used to get on my nerves but . . . now. It's like a little postcard from home, and I ask myself why did I drink so much last night?

Beat.

April   You're quiet.

Gordon   And I know exactly how James felt under her gaze.

I open my mouth and out comes . . .

'Let's go to the fair.'

Sid   I tell the Big Cheese I'm going to walk the rest of the way with Neil. As we get near home Mum pulls up and she's so busy fussing that I'm not happy, and that we need to move away that she drives into the back of a Range Rover. Me and Neil get in and we help her get the car back home. She's flapping about the bumper but Dad's there, so I go upstairs and I'm not sure if Neil's allowed upstairs or not. So we both stop. I'm on the stairs looking back and he's in the hall looking up. It's up to us to make the rules. I check where Mum is and she's on the phone exaggerating to someone about the bump. I decide, if I tap my hip and he gets it, he can come.

Sid *taps his hip, and smiles.*

He likes upstairs.

Beat.

Later on she's back on track. And in counselling mode. She bought this book on grief from Amazon and every time she's finished a chapter she tries to get me to do stuff.

Beat.

Today, it's finishing sentences.

Beat.

I sit with my head on the kitchen table and with Neil at my feet.

April   It can be anything Sid. What's important is, we don't hold back do we?

Sid *shrugs.*

April   'I wish I had . . .'

Sid   I don't know.

April   Try Sid, it'll help you.

Sid   I wish I had a gadget to tell me when to speak and when to look meaningful.

Beat.

I look away because I can't look at her and hurt her at the same time. She keeps the book on her lap and tries to thumb through it without me seeing.

April   Okay. Why don't you tell me what you want to talk about?

Sid *has nothing to say.*

Go on? It can be anything.

Sid   I look at her. Why does she want to own this? Of all things, she wants to get her claws into this.

'How about, my three best friends die, I'm half blind, I don't remember anything and my Mum buys me a fucking dog? What's that about?'

April   I thought you'd like a dog.

Sid   'I've never wanted a dog in my life. When have I said, I want a dog? When have I ever said I like dogs? It's the last thing I want. It's the stupidest thing anyone's ever bought me in my entire life.'

I find myself reassuring Neil with my foot. Mum suggests I'm angry about other things, not Neil. I tell her I'm angry about the Big Cheese blaming Alex for crashing the car.

Beat.

April   How about we try some more sentences now?

Sid *would rather die.*

'The thing I miss about the boys is . . .'

Sid I'm on the brink of walking out but I get the faintest, the faintest whiff, of a dog fart. In the middle of all this, Neil has decided to drop a stinker. And why not? He's amongst friends, he's had a nice walk, he's relaxed. I don't know why but breathing in his fart chills me out a bit.

'The thing I miss about the boys is missing the boys.'

April I feel . . .

Sid I feel left out.

I realise Mum doesn't care what I'm saying, but that I'm saying something is all that matters. It's like the reverse of her with me, I don't hear her but I know she's there. And for the first time in ages, I'm there with my Mum.

When she kicks off later about some mud, I make sure she knows I appreciate her.

Gordon I *hate* the May fair. The noise, the litter, it lowers the tone. But tonight I can't get enough of it. April doesn't know where to look; I buy candyfloss, fizzy pop. I see Sid and Luke with a bunch of girls.

'Ahoy!'

Sid *freezes with embarrassment.*

Gordon See if . . . see if you can beat your old man on the strongman?

And I do a, a sort of a jig.

Gordon *is embarrassed.*

Sid Nah, we're waiting for/ mates.

Gordon Tenner if you can beat me?

'Deal!' says Luke and he swipes the tenner out of my hand. On the way to the stall he grabs my bicep.

'Don't fancy your chances Mr W.' I can't take my eyes off April. We get to the strongman and she sidles up.

April (*side of mouth*)   'What are you doing?'

Gordon   Bit of fun, relax.

But as Sid peels off his jumper I think I don't know what I'm doing. April doesn't want this, Sid doesn't want this, and I don't. Luke is like a pig in shit, with everyone watching. Sid hits the bell straight away. I go next and hit the bell, but it's not as loud as Sid's. We have two more goes each and the third time Sid is warmed up and nearly takes the bell off. Whereas my third time, I'm exhausted and don't even ring the bell. I can barely hold the hammer.

April   Well done Sid! My big strong boy.

Sid   Another go Dad? Double or quits?

Gordon   No/ thank you.

Sid   Go on. I'll only use one hand.

Gordon   I want to say, 'Well done, have fun' . . . but I say:

'Have a bit more grace in future Sid.'

He looks at me and his smile fades. April is speechless. She gives him another note and tells him to go and buy some chips. He rejoins his friends waving the money.

April   What was that about?

Gordon   I don't know. Just a bit of fatherly advice, I can advise my son if I want can't I?

And I find myself pulling her by the hips and kissing her. I don't know what's wrong with me, perhaps it's all the riled up teenagers but tonight I have a real appetite for her.

April   Stop it. I'm. People can see. Gordon!

Gordon   I can see she's thrilled though.

'What do you want? Choose something? Anything.'

April   Oh I don't want any of this old rubbish.

Gordon   I grab her from behind and kiss her neck, it's like she's one of the fairground attractions.

'I want to win something for you, tell me what you want and I'll win it for you.'

April   It's crap!

Gordon   Let me win something for you.

Beat.

Anything.

April *slowly points at something.*

April   I want that one then.

Gordon   A bloody reindeer!

Beat.

After three goes, April loses patience.

April   Come on. Let's get a cup of tea.

Gordon   I want the reindeer.

April   Forget about the bloody reindeer, you'll never get it.

Gordon   I buy another two goes.

April   Gordon. I am bored.

Gordon   I take aim and

April huffs.

I take aim again and this time she says

April   I'm going to find Ronnie.

Gordon   I'm trying to win you something here?

But she walks off through the fairground through all the lights. In my head I follow her, and we buy some tea and put whisky in it and we run behind a trailer and kiss. But all I do is turn to the man and say:

'Keep giving me darts till I'm the winner.'

*

April   After inspecting the car, Gordon 'helps' unpack. In Gordon's world, helping means moving things around until he finds something he can open and eat immediately.

I open the fridge and the light comes on and it's the first time I realise how dark it is in the kitchen. I stand there, looking at the fridge holding an Edam cheese and I have no idea what I'm doing. There's a fridge full of food, I don't know if it's fresh or old, I don't know if I should be pulling things out or putting things in, I don't know if I've bought this cheese or just pulled it out. I know I should be at the fridge, but why I don't know.

With the cheese in my hand I look at Gordon.

'What I am doing with this?'

Gordon   You've had a shock with the airbag, why don't I run you a bath? Have some peace and quiet.

April   Why am I holding this cheese like an idiot?

Gordon stops leaning and straightens up, alarmed at my tone. I stand there trying for the life of me to work out why I have a cheese in my hand; it's like the most complicated sum in the world. I focus and concentrate and just stare at the cheese. No matter how hard I try, I can't do it. For a second I think I'm having a stroke.

And then I hear a voice; in the distance it's not clear at first but the more I concentrate the better I hear it. I look at Gordon and from his face I can see that the voice is actually mine.

'If it wasn't for Sid I'd leave you.'

Sid   Neil and I are walking around the lanes and I see the Big Cheese going into his house. I tie Neil up and I'm banging on his door. The Big Cheese answers and he's holding a scotch egg. How quick can you get in the house, take your shoes off and get a scotch egg?

When **Sid** *speaks as the Big Cheese he holds the scotch egg to his chest.*

He's all trying to get me to come in and stuff.

'Nah. I've, I've uh got Neil with me.' He like leans out of his house;

Sid *does this.*

He sees Neil. 'Well. What can I do for you Sid?' 'I think the speeding foundation's a fucking crap idea.' I walk around when I talk to him, but I don't care.

Sid *walks around.*

'The boys would have hated it. Especially Luke.' 'I'm sorry you think that Sid, but I don't agree.'

Sid *points a finger at the Big Cheese.*

'I know them, you don't.' 'I know you're upset Sid so let's calm down. What do you suggest would be a fitting tribute?'

'Fitting tribute? There is no fitting tribute,' I say. 'I don't want a fitting tribute.' The Big Cheese blinks. 'We have to do something.' I realise I've been a bit out of line with him.

It's just normally, in this situation Luke would have said something sarcy, Owen would have tried to calm everyone down, Alex would have been looking the wrong way and I would have waited till the fighting started. But now it's just me, and I've got to weigh up all my feelings all the time on my own. I don't know what to do. He tries again. 'We have to change something so this never happens again and no one has to go through what we have.' 'I don't know.'

'What would you like to change?'

'Why don't you get the council to get Pizza Hut to come here? Or a bowling alley? Or a McDonalds? McDonalds would be good, somewhere we can go that doesn't chuck people out for making a coffee last three hours.' 'Your three

best friends die. And you want a McDonalds?' Even I get
how stupid that sounds. Before I can think I'm at it again.

Sid *searches for the words.*

'The reason we're all killing ourselves driving to Hereford
or Kiddie is because there's fuck all for us in this town. It
isn't Alex's fault. It's yours. It's shit being a kid here. But
you won't do anything about it because you'd rather some
cunt from London come here and spend twenty quid on a
cheddar than open a place for us.' 'I'm sorry Sid that's not
true.' 'You lot love tourists more than kids and that's why all
my mates are dead and I'm half blind.' 'That's not true at all
Sid, why don't you come in and we'll talk some more.' I see
my reflection in his glasses and I look tiny. 'I've got the dog,'
and I turn around.

Beat.

I untie Neil. I don't wanna wave to him but I do and he
raises . . .

Beat.

He raises his scotch egg to me the prick.

April Sid managed about ten minutes of counselling. The
idea of being alone with Gordon sends me into a panic so I
throw myself into some marking, he knows not to disturb me
when I'm marking. I don't mark a single book, but when he
comes in from the garage I act like I'm heavily into it.

Gordon No serious damage done.

April I've got a lot to get through.

I watch him through the corner of my eye and he looks
around for something to do. Something to be near me. He
starts to load the dishwasher. And he does it just as I like
to do it, glasses and cutlery first. I stop marking and look
up and there he is tensed up trying to pull the drawer out
further without making any noise.

April   Gordon?

Gordon   Yes.

April   I want to tell him why I said what I said.

Long pause.

'Big plates at the back.'

He obeys quietly and I feel sorry for him. But before I can do anything, Sid comes back from one of his walks with Neil. Even though he's like a yo-yo he moves so silently and inoffensively these days. He heads to his bedroom. For some reason I decide to make a big song and dance about the mud they've walked into the corridor, so I start, huffing and puffing.

Standing at the bottom of the stairs Sid doesn't move as I get on my hands and knees and start scrubbing. My spine chills as he doesn't go up the stairs but goes into the kitchen. He comes into the corridor, dunks a cloth in the bucket and starts scrubbing the carpet behind me.

April   No, no don't bother, I'll do it.

And I push him off the stain he's scrubbing. He straightens himself on his haunches.

Sid   I can do it.

April   No you can't.

Sid   It's my fault.

Pause.

April   I want my lazy son back. My stroppy boy who'll happily watch me scrub up his mess while he plays on his Xbox. I don't want a son who understands consequence.

Beat.

'You're not well. I'll do it.'

He starts again, twitching his head like a bird. He does this when he's trying to focus. As I crawl over to Sid, Gordon comes in.

Please stop.

Pause.

Please stop.

Sid   It's okay.

April   Please.

Sid   I don't mind.

April   I don't want you to do this.

Sid   It's coming off see.

April   I need you to stop, you're making it worse, just leave me alone to clean my carpet. I wish everyone would just leave me to clean my carpet the way I want to.

Sid *is confused.* **April** *is ashamed.*

Gordon   Let your Mum do the carpet.

Pause.

Sid   I'm old enough.

April *closes her eyes in pain.*

Gordon   I know. Just, let's leave her.

April   I don't look up as Gordon ushers Sid out of the corridor.

Gordon   I'll run you a bath.

April*'s heart sinks.*

Sid   Neil and I stand by the river at the bottom of the Linney.

Beat.

I see myself in the water. That's me now. That's me. A one-eyed boy with three friends missing. I throw stones and mud and sticks in. But in this town's water, that's all I'll ever be. A one-eyed boy with three friends missing.

April I light candles, put some music on and sink into the bath. As I unwind, the music acts as a thermal to my thoughts and they float around a night a few weeks ago like a glider.

Beat.

'I want to get high,' I say and sink under the water trying to hide, as I hold Sid's bong towards Dean in his council flat with the furniture too big. I drift towards him with a fifty-pound note. 'You know how to operate this don't you?' The steam from the bath looks like smoke, and with an unstoppable smile I tell Dean I avoid the other boys' mothers now.

Reaching for the razor, Ronnie Trott carves up the town to avoid seeing Mark and his new fling and I think I can't avoid my lounge.

I lather up my soap and I lean over the side of Dean's sofa, and throw up on to an oven tray:

'Do you know who Gordon's sleeping with?'

I refill the bath with fresh hot water and float towards the night of the crash. I sit alone at the Symphony Hall and watch the couple in front share a drink. Anthony sings under a gauze sheet, and I cry through every song, I'm so perfectly alone. I think I'd like to paint him; this woman trapped in a six-foot New York man's body.

Beat.

'He had to climb over his friends to get out,' the officer says. We were so lucky.

Beat.

Strip lights give me hospital jet lag and I've travelled nowhere. The One We Take To America is in Gordon's boot. Half way through a song the sheet falls from Anthony, and everyone cheers even though I'm alone and cold, in the car park, holding a photo of my family.

Below the waterline I try to escape but it's as if a sheet falls off *me*, and now I can see.

(*Beat.*)

The tap drips and it's like it's applauding me: it's not me who's trapped. It's Gordon. I'm not angry with him for trying to leave. I'm angry with him for trying to stay.

Gordon   'What's the most amount of cash I can withdraw on my account?'

Beat.

I look at Katie the teller, and she can see I'm on some kind of mission. Only I don't know what it's for.

Beat.

I drop the money into a holdall of Sid's and leave the branch.

Beat.

Two hours later I'm standing in a purpose-built flat in Smethwick with a letting agent. 'Where do I sign?'

Beat.

I sit on the bed next to the holdall and look around the furnished flat. My new flat. I walk around getting to know the IKEA-trite furniture. It's soulless, and for some reason I feel completely at home. I lie back on the bed with my hands tucked behind my head.

Beat.

This is different to the B&Bs; this is going to be quiet.
Anonymous. No April, no Sid, no cider festival, no parking
campaigns, no town hall meetings, no pub, no May fair. Just
me. Peace and quiet.

Gordon *pulls a phone out and puts it to his ear.*

Andrew?

Beat.

Gordon.

Beat.

Walker.

Beat.

I've done it.

Beat.

(*Hopeful.*) Where are you?

Beat.

You think. You think you might like to come over? I'll stock
the minibar. Or, fridge, as we call it in Smethwick.

Beat.

Gordon *hangs his head.*

Okay.

Gordon *hangs up.*

April   For the first time in years I feel like drawing.

Beat.

I rub a face on the steamed-up mirror.

Gordon   On the drive home, I list all the things I'm going
to pack. Shirts, trousers, underwear, toiletries, slippers.

I need the big suitcase down, the One We Take To America. Some favourite books and DVDs and I know exactly which photograph I'm taking. The three of us in Tenby.

I pull into the driveway, and the boys are in the garage lifting weights. It's the last time I see them together.

Beat.

Sid stands over Owen as he bench presses, Sid's the guru when it comes to anything sporty, everyone defers to him.

Beat.

I watch them for a while. Alex, such a thoughtful young chap, calls out to the boys to pack it in, he sees me waiting to put the car in.

'It's fine; it's fine lads, you carry on.'

'Just getting the guns pumped for the girls in town Mr W,' shouts Luke and shows me a bicep.

'As long as that's all you're pumping Luke.'

And the boys guffaw, Sid springs into action and takes the bar off Owen.

You've never seen four boys like it. Like puppies, from the same litter. I don't think they had any secrets between them.

(*Beat.*)

Sid   Mum's gone to see Anthony and Johnsons in Birmingham. She's left cottage pie.

Gordon   Good good. I'd forgotten.

I want to tell Sid everything, I want to say I can't do any more for you.

(*Beat.*)

I salute the boys as they pull off for the last time, music blaring, Alex's exhaust pipe blowing.

I hear a surge of laughter as they vanish around the hedge.

And I think.

(*Long pause.*)

I think: thank God they've gone.

Sid   At the riverbank, a gentle breeze takes me back to a morning not long before.

Beat.

Alex picks me up first on the way.

'What the fuck's with the gay hair?'

'It's not gay.'

Sid *fiddles with his hair.*

(*To himself.*) It's not gay.

Luke gets in.

'Sid's hair's gone gay.'

Sid *punches Alex on the leg.*

Luke says:

(*Camp voice.*) 'Well I think it's lovely.'

Sid *leans back and gives Luke a dead leg.*

'Don't you start!'

Alex laughs and bangs the steering wheel. 'Football kit! Shit!' says Luke.

'Fucking hell,' says Alex and we turn around and head back to Luke's. Outside his I say:

'Luke mate.'

'What mate?'

'Get us a beenie mate.'

We pick up Owen, and he starts telling us about who he was Facebooking last night. He's rubbish around girls but get him online and he's a genius.

Beat.

I roll down the window, I'm not sure why. But with the beenie on, the banter and the boys, I want the whole town to see us. I want the whole town to lean out of their little houses and see us. Just see us, for once.

Gordon   I look at the paraphernalia and wrack my brain; when did I agree to this?

April   I think we should get Sid a dog. I think he needs a friend.

Gordon (*distracted reading paper*)   Oh yes.

April   Do you think it's a good idea?

Gordon (*distracted reading paper*)   Uh-huh.

There's a basket, a dog bowl, dog-gate, dog-toy, dog food. And in front of me, in the middle of the lounge, is a panting dog.

Sid looks like he's on camera, he doesn't know what to do with his arms, and I want to pick up all the stuff, and the dog, and throw it all out the front door and say to Sid:

'It was a crap idea, you do what you want. Whatever you need to do we'll do too.'

But I don't. I say:

'Get up off the sofa and stroke the dog.'

Pause.

Sid's patting him like he's bouncing a ball and I find myself gathering all the dog stuff together, putting it all in the basket so it's easy to carry to the car when this goes pear-shaped.

Beat.

I pick up the dog-gate and the mechanism swings open and the way I'm holding it, it sort of frames Sid, April and the dog, like they're in a photo. And I remember speaking to a fireman, who was there at the scene. He said Sid surviving was a 'miracle'. My boy.

'Uh, what are we going to call him then?'

Sid   Neil?

April   Neil?

Gordon   Neil it is! Welcome Neil, I'm Gordon, Walker, this is April, and this is Sid and this is your new home. Hey?

And I stroke the dog like I find him adorable.

(*Long pause.*)

Because what's better? Lying to get what you want; or lying so people you *love* can get what they want?

Sid   The breeze dies and Neil lets me know it's time to go by circling around and not saying anything. Just as Mum does. And I think of her in the kitchen, in her own little square of the world wringing her hands, and I realise without me around she feels pointless. Just like I feel with the boys gone. But it's worse for her, because she can't grieve what isn't dead. I've been a ghost to her ever since the crash.

Scene Two

Sid *is off-stage.*

April *folds shirts and puts them on the table.*

Gordon *is on the phone with some paperwork on the table.*

Gordon   Yes.

Beat.

Yes it's a VW Polo.

Beat.

The integrity of the bumper is fine, there's no damage that I can see. My wife was driving.

Yes she drove into the back of a stationary vehicle.

Beat.

Yes. It's just that the airbag has been decommissioned. Commissioned – I'm not sure what the right term is. The airbag's gone off.

Beat.

No. I don't mind.

Gordon *picks at some food.*

Yes. Hello. I was telling your colleague, my wife was driving our VW Polo earlier today and bumped into a stationary car. And the airbag has been decommissioned or commissioned, what's the right term?

Yes.

It's gone off. The airbag went off.

Beat.

The bumper doesn't need replacing but obviously the airbag does and I can't see anything referring to it in our policy.

Beat.

Okay I'll hold.

Yes?

Beat.

Hang on.

Gordon *gets some of the paperwork together.*

It's Alpha Zebra one three nine nine Lima Papa.

Beat.

Walker.

Beat.

Gordon *sees* **April** *stack up his shirts into a pile.*

Uh. Sorry?

Beat.

Yes.

Gordon *goes through some more paperwork, but he can't stop watching* **April** *fold shirts.*

Gordon (*to* **April**)   What are you doing?

April *ignores him.*

VW Polo.

Beat.

Yes I'll hold.

Gordon *eats something and looks at his paperwork.* **April** *watches him.*

Silence.

April   Do you remember that purple pashmina Sid gave me for my birthday?

(*In response to* **Gordon**'s *reaction.*)

The/ shawl.

Gordon   The wrap thing yes.

April   I've been looking for it for months haven't I?

Gordon   Yes, we couldn't let on, we thought you'd lost it.

April   I turned the house upside down looking for it didn't I? The last time I wore it we went to that picnic-in-the-park concert in Berrington Hall, do you remember?

Gordon   Yes.

April   That's the last time I wore it.

Gordon   Do you think we left it there then? It's probably gone by now.

April   The night of the crash at the hospital I was stood outside making phone calls and I got cold. I was walking back and forth trying to stay warm and it hit me. I knew exactly where that pashmina was.

April *pulls a suitcase out, The One We Take To America, and puts* **Gordon***'s shirts in as she speaks.*

Gordon   Where was it?

Beat.

April   Folded up, under the plastic sheet. In the boot of your car.

April *picks up a photograph of the family, places it on his folded shirts and closes the suitcase.*

Gordon *fills with dread.*

Gordon *puts his head in his hands.*

April   I saw it. I saw your packed suitcase.

Gordon   It's . . . I can / explain.

April   Don't you dare stay with us because of what happened to Sid.

Gordon   I . . . It's. I can make it.

Gordon *censors himself as* **Sid** *enters the room oblivious to the weird atmosphere.* **Gordon** *can't take his eyes off* **April***, who turns her back to both of them.*

Slowly it dawns on **Sid** *that something is the matter.*

Sid   Is everything okay?

Deafening silence from his parents.

Gordon   Everything's fine.

Gordon *waves his phone.*

We're just, just a bit shaken up about the airbag. Aren't we love?

Very long silence as **April** *stares at the floor, unwilling to hurt* **Sid***, unable to lie any more.*

Gordon   Where's Neil?

Sid (*looking at* **April**)   Basket.

April *can't look at either of them.* **Sid** *is really unnerved.*

Gordon   Where've you been then? Give him a good walk did you? Neil.

Sid *is torn between* **Gordon** *and* **April***.*

Sid   Um . . . yeah.

Gordon *is out of conversation.*

Sid *watches* **April***. He turns to* **Gordon***, points to* **April** *and indicates 'what's up with her?'*

Gordon *can't begin to explain.*

Sid *turns to his Mum, he thinks about leaving . . . but stops himself.*

Sid (*to* **April**)   I was wondering, Mum . . . if, if you could help me, with my eye?

April *turns, and sees* **Sid** *looking at her.*

After some fumbling, **Sid** *gets his drops out and holds them towards her.*

April*'s knees weaken and she has to steady herself. This is the best present she could have wished for.*

April   Yes. Yes all right.

She takes the drops from **Sid***'s hand.*

April *and* **Gordon**'s *eyes meet momentarily.*

Sid *tilts his head back, she attempts to administer the drops but it's unsuccessful. They shuffle around each other, it's awkward.*

April   Hang on. Sit down.

Sid *obeys and takes a seat.* **April** *stands behind him and holds his face close to her body.*

She looks down at him while he looks up at her.

Gordon   Do you uh, do you need some light? To see.

April *looks at the room lighting, it's not good enough.*

April   That might help.

Gordon *pulls down the pendant light above the table so it stretches down and he angles it over* **April**'s *shoulder to light* **Sid**'s *face.*

April *sits down on the bench, and she indicates for* **Sid** *to rest his head on her lap.*

April   Come here.

Sid *stretches out and lies on his mother's lap.*

Sid (*to* **April**)   Remember that time you knocked your sewing box over and the needles went all over the carpet, and he comes in and says, 'I'll get my magnet.'

April *and* **Sid** *laugh.*

In perfect silence, **April** *administers the drops.*

Sid *blinks.*

April *looks at* **Sid**'s *eye for a while – she's evidently avoided looking at it for so long.*

She applies another drop, **Sid** *blinks and the job is done.*

April   Do you want me to keep this safe?

Sid *nods.*

April *looks around briefly for somewhere to put it but doesn't want to disturb* **Sid***; without a second thought* **Gordon** *offers a hand and* **April** *instinctively gives it to him.* **Gordon** *puts the drops in his pocket and* **April** *returns to looking at her son.*

Gently, **April** *wipes the solution from* **Sid***'s face.*

Gordon *puts his hand on* **April***'s shoulder.*

April *kisses* **Sid** *on the nose.*

Lights down.

The End.